D0758846

♥ You're a magic mate ♥

Thank you for your love and laughter!

ℛℛ
RAVETTE PUBLISHING

First published in 2008 by
Ravette Publishing Ltd
Unit 3, Tristar Centre, Star Road
Partridge Green, West Sussex RH13 8RA

www.juicylucydesigns.com

ISBN: 978-1-84161-305-5

You are an angel

and a special friend

a little magic
wish for you.

..you spread joy

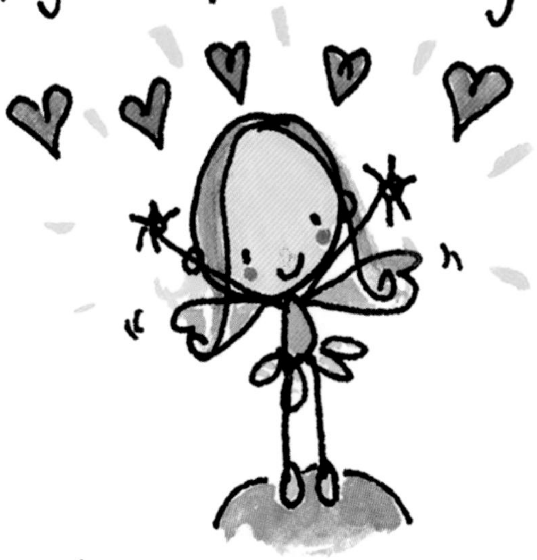

wherever you go..

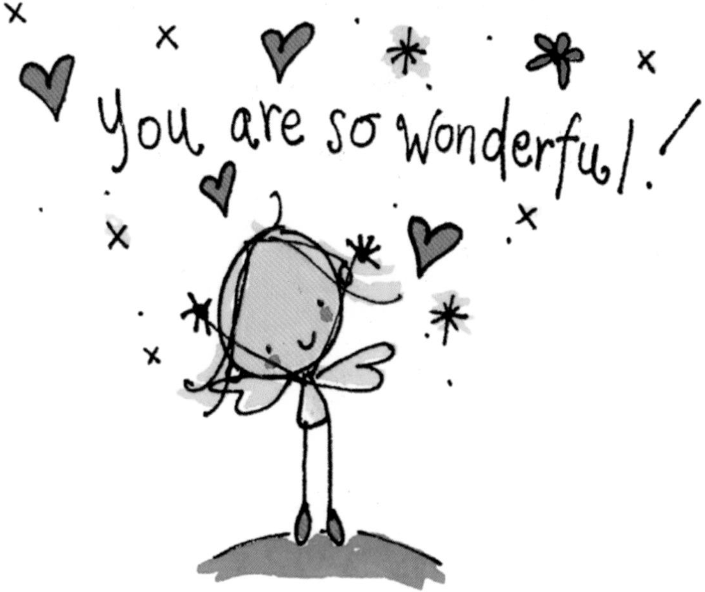
You are so wonderful!

thank-you for being

* you! *

I'm so proud of you!

.. You're the best thing since sliced bread..

Have a day filled
with joy!

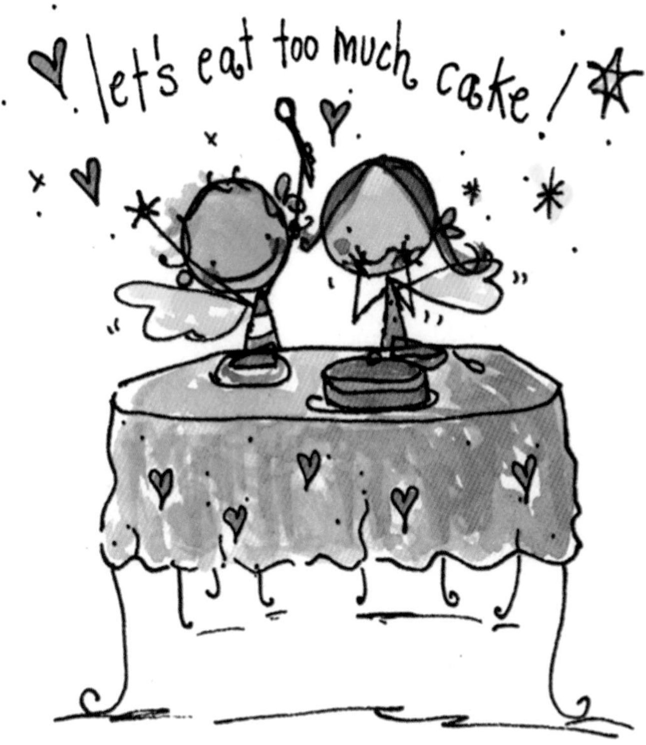
let's eat too much cake!

the
little
fairies
think
you
are rather
Special!

Professional shoppers

..Party Princesses!

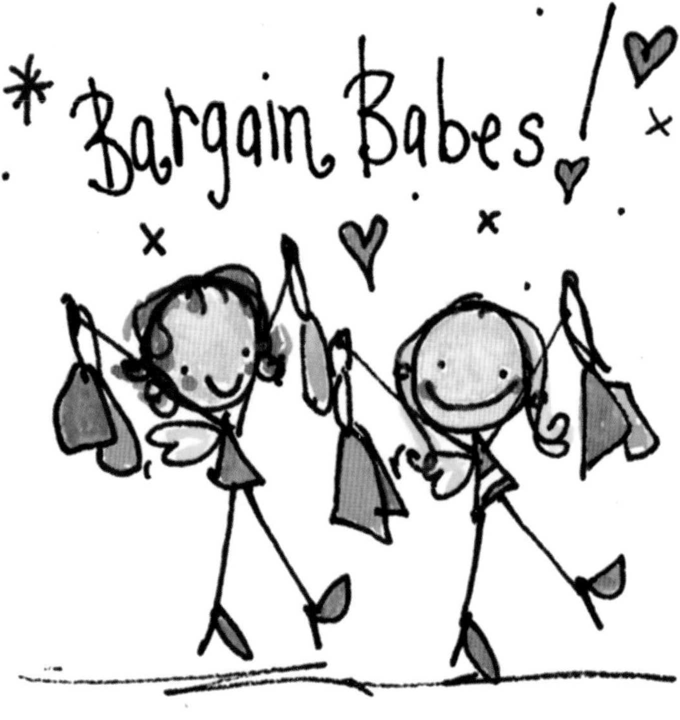
Bargain Babes!

for a truly special mate...

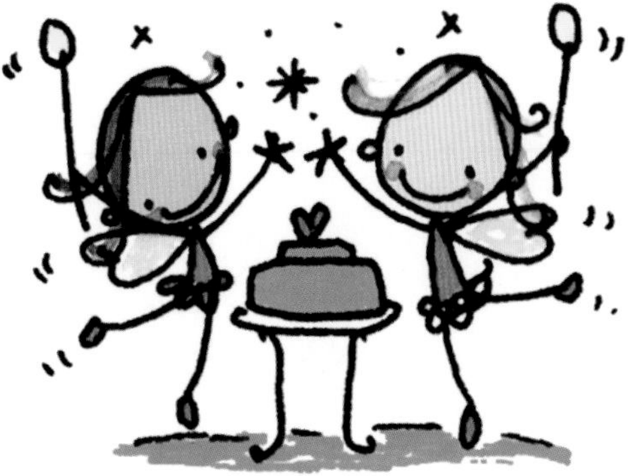

let's fill our face with tons of cake!

you are surrounded

by love x

Twinkle, twinkle

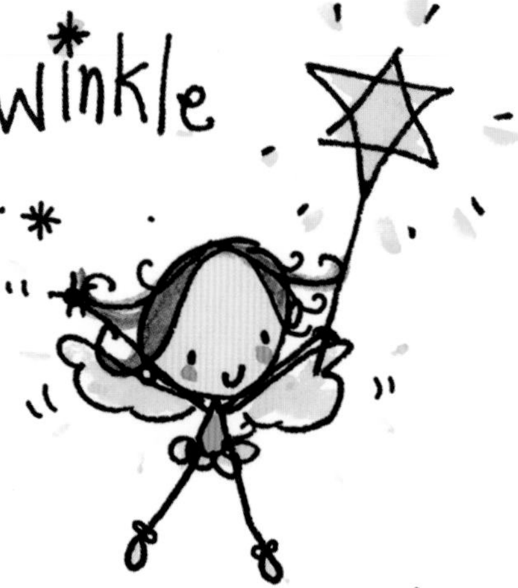

You're a star!

always there in times of need!

Thank-you
fairy
much !

Hello Fairy Princess

♥ ..Hurrah! ♥

✳ ..let's have some fun! ✳

all the little fairies told me that you should eat as much cake as you like!

x

I love you so much I could squish you.

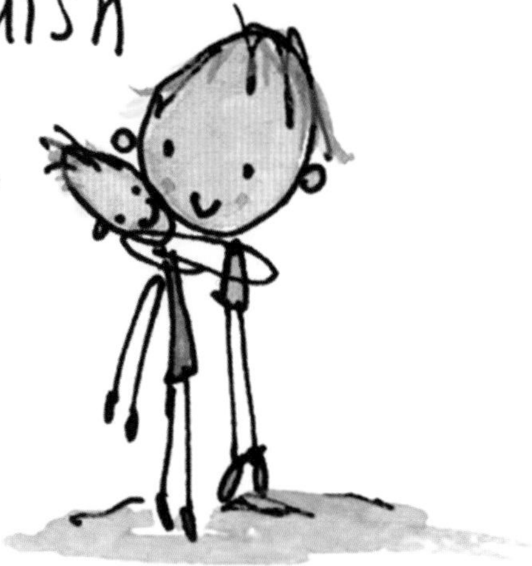

..this little hug is for you..

let's drink tea + eat cake!

The little fairies love you!

·you're a great mate!

♡ ..Thank-you for everything.. ♡

..The little angels

love you x ..

You make such a difference in the world.

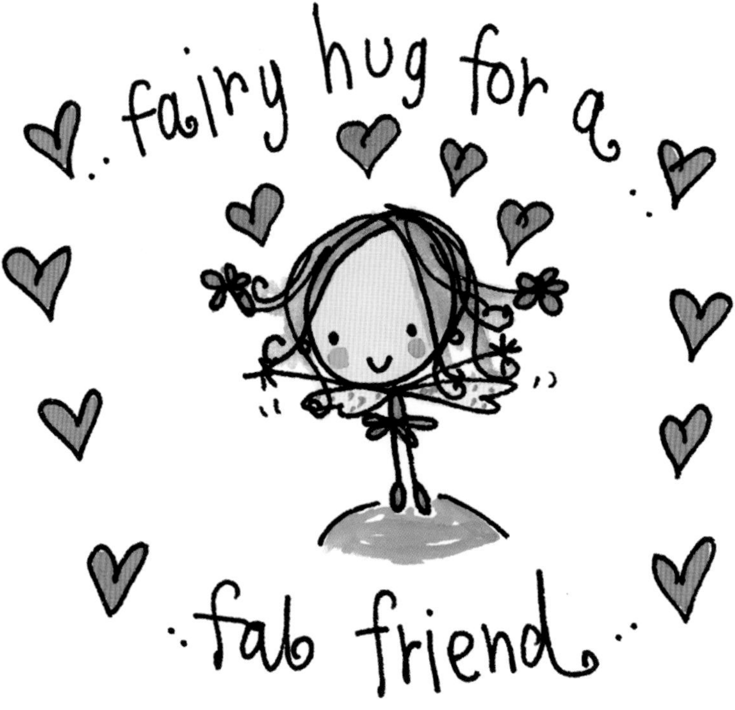
fairy hug for a
fab friend

The little fairies think that you are
beautiful and special and kind!
They are thrilled that you have this book,
and want you to know that the lovely
people at Ravette have also published ...

	ISBN	**Price**
I love you	978-1-84161-298-0	£4.99
I love you Mum!	978-1-84161-300-0	£4.99
Let's be rudie nudies	978-1-84161-299-7	£4.99

HOW TO ORDER   Please send a cheque/postal order in £ sterling, made payable to 'Ravette Publishing' for the cover price of the books and allow the following for post & packaging ...

UK & BFPO   70p for the first book & 40p per book thereafter
Europe & Eire   £1.30 for the first book & 70p per book thereafter
Rest of the world £2.20 for the first book & £1.10 per book thereafter

RAVETTE PUBLISHING LTD

Unit 3 Tristar Centre, Star Road, Partridge Green, West Sussex RH13 8RA
Tel: 01403 711443   Fax: 01403 711554   Email: ravettepub@aol.com

Prices and availability are subject to change without prior notice.